THE SEVENTH DAY

The Story of the Jewish Sabbath

by Miriam Chaikin

WOODCUTS BY DAVID FRAMPTON

DOUBLEDAY & COMPANY, INC.
GARDEN CITY, NEW YORK

Thanks are due to Rabbi Deborah Prinz
for her sensitive reading of the manuscript.

Library of Congress Cataloging in Publication Data

Chaikin, Miriam.
The seventh day.

SUMMARY: A narrative version of the Old Testament
passages describing how the Jewish Sabbath came to be.
    1. Bible stories, English—O. T. Pentateuch.
2. Sabbath—Juvenile literature. [1. Bible stories—
O.T. 2. Sabbath] I. Frampton, David. II. Title.
        BS551.2.C45   222'.1'09505
      ISBN: 0-385-14919-0 Trade
          0-385-14920-4 Prebound
Library of Congress Catalog Card Number 78–22789

First Edition

For my brother, Joseph Chaikin, with love

Rather than being a time of deprivation, of doing without, the Sabbath is for observant Jews the most joyous holiday of all and a time for celebration. The cares of daily life are set aside and a new, spiritual life is entered into as they keep this covenant with the Lord and praise creation. For them, the Sabbath is the queen of days and they, rich and poor alike, are king.

THE SEVENTH DAY

The Story of the Jewish Sabbath

God first made the world. It was dark and watery, and God saw that the darkness was incomplete, and made light. The light was good, it parted the darkness, and God liked it, and God called the darkness night and the light day, and that was the First Day.

God found the waters too much and too many, rising up above the world and descending far below it, and God parted the waters, creating above a great space, and God liked the space and called it heaven, and the day and night that saw heaven, that was the Second Day.

And the waters covered the world, and the land was hidden, and God assembled the waters, making them to come together, and causing land to appear. And God liked the land and called it earth, and God gave the earth seed, to bring forth plants and herbs and grasses and fruit-bearing trees, each with seed of its own, to create its own kind, and the day and night that saw the living earth, that was the Third Day.

9

God looked at the heaven, which was so far empty, and put in it two great lights, one to rule the night, the other to rule the day, and put in it also many lesser lights, which God called stars, and the lights lit up the earth and were good, and they could mark order in the days and weeks and years and seasons, and the day and night that saw the lights of heaven, that was the Fourth Day.

And God filled the waters, which God called seas, and in them made creatures, kinds to live in the deep and kinds that could fly, each with seed, to create its own kind, and they all had as food the herbs and grasses which the earth put forth, and God saw that the creation was good, and liked it, and the day and night that saw the living sea, that was the Fifth Day.

And God made a multitude of creatures to live on the earth, kinds to roam and walk and creep upon it, and gave all of them seed, to create their own kind, and all had as food the herbs and grasses which the earth put forth, and the creation was good and God liked it.

Then God made the last creation, out of the dust of the red earth; in God's own image, God created human beings, both male and female, and gave them seed, to create their own kind, and God breathed into their nostrils and gave them the breath of life, and the male and female were Adam and Eve, and all the earth was theirs, and God blessed them, saying, Be fruitful and multiply, and populate the earth, and God gave them power over all creation and commanded them to take care of the earth and keep it fertile.

Then God beheld all that had been created, and saw the order that was in it, and saw that each thing was good, and that all things were good together, and that all creatures had food to eat, and God liked it very much, and the day and night that saw the work of creation completed, that was the Sixth Day.

The next day was the Seventh Day, and on it God rested, God blessed the Seventh Day as a day of rest, and called it holy, and God named it the day to honor creation, and this was a commandment.

The creation that God had made was good, and the seas heaved with life, and fish leapt out of the waters and back into them, and fowl flapped their wings in the air and beasts roamed and ran upon the earth, and the land put forth a multitude of plants and trees whose fruit was good to eat and a delight to behold, and the land was a garden.

And in the garden were Adam and Eve, put there by God to tend it and dress it, and the sweetness of all creation was theirs, and their eyes and ears told them so

and all their senses knew it, and they delighted in it and lived in bliss. Yet they looked aside and disobeyed God, for God had told them that they could eat all the fruit of the garden, but not the fruit of the two trees in the center of the garden.

The fruit of those trees was forbidden to them, and the trees were the tree of eternal life and the tree of judgment, and it was not part of God's design that man should eat of them, and though God had forbidden Adam and Eve to eat of those two trees, they ate the fruit of the tree of judgment, and bliss that had been theirs was lost to them and they felt naked and ashamed.

Lest they eat also of the tree of eternal life, God banished Adam and Eve from the garden and caused the earth to bring forth thorns and thistles, that they should have to toil to eat of it, and God reminded them that they were created out of the earth and told them they would return to it at the end of their days, saying, Of the earth are you made and to earth shall you return.

And Adam and Eve went out of the garden, they departed from the garden and began to populate the earth, and the lights of heaven marked the passage of time, and children were born and grew old, and men and women became many.

Though they became many, only a few loved God and walked in God's ways, for the multitude was corrupt and did evil, and God repented of creation and sent a flood to wipe it out.

But Noah and his wife, who were righteous and

14

An Israelite woman rescued her infant son, she hid him in a basket at the edge of the river, and he was found by the pharaoh's daughter, who gave him the name Moses and kept him for her own son.

Moses lived among Egyptians, but his mother and Miriam, his sister, were known to him, and he knew he was an Israelite, and as he grew to manhood it angered him to see his people enslaved, and when he came upon an Egyptian beating an Israelite, he killed the man.

The Egyptian king was angered and sought Moses to slay him, but Moses fled to the land of Midian where he lived, and he married Zipporah there, the daughter of Jethro, the priest, and he became a shepherd of Jethro's flock.

As Moses was tending his flock one day God spoke to him from a flaming bush and called him by name, and Moses hid his face from the greatness that was the Lord and answered, Here am I, and God spoke to Moses, saying, I am the God of your fathers, and I have heard the cries of the children who are slaves in Egypt. Those who sought your life are no more. Go there, and bring out the children of Israel, and take them to the land I have given you.

Moses, being slow of speech and a stammerer, questioned how one such as he could persuade the pharaoh to let the people go free, and asked also why he had been chosen, and God answered, Fear not, I will be with you, and God told Moses to let Aaron, his brother, speak for him, and instructed Moses in what to say and

18

gave him signs to show and wonders to perform, that all might know he had spoken with the Lord.

Moses told Aaron of God's words, and they went before the council of elders and spoke to them, and when those assembled learned that God had heard the cries of the children of Israel, they bowed down their heads and wept with joy.

20

Moses set his wife and sons upon asses and he and Aaron and the other lords and nobles with them journeyed to Egypt, where Moses pleaded with the pharaoh to let the Israelites go, and when the pharaoh refused, Moses performed the wonders God had given him to perform, afflicting the Egyptians with plagues and punishments, until the pharaoh was forced to let the Israelites go.

After four hundred and thirty years of having lived in Egypt, the Israelites, some six hundred thousand men, women, and children, left Rameses on foot, they and their flocks and herds and oxen, and their tents, and all their houscholds. And Moscs camc before them, and said, Remember this day, when the Lord with a mighty arm brought you out of Egypt, where you were slaves, and made you free.

And the Israelites gave thanks to the Lord and sang praises to God's name and they went out into the wilderness and began their journey toward Canaan, the land God had given to their ancestors, and that was theirs, and God went before them to show them the way, appearing by day as a pillar of cloud and by night as a pillar of fire, taking them not through the land of the Philistines, which was near, but over the wilderness, to try them and test them.

They pitched their tents and encamped near the Red Sea and, instructed by Moses, they pitched a tent of meeting outside the camp that God might be worshipped there. But when evening fell the scouts arrived

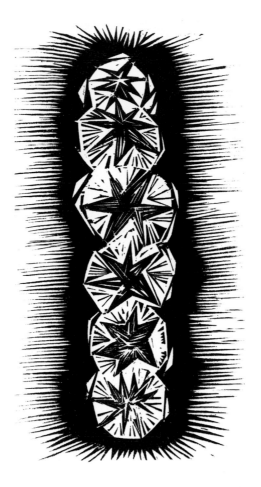

at the camp and the people came out of their tents to listen and they heard the scouts tell Moses that the pharaoh had repented of his decision to let the Israelites go free, and that Egyptian soldiers on horses and in chariots were on the way to kill them.

Downcast, the people returned to their tents and began to murmur, saying, It would have been better to remain as slaves in Egypt than to die in the wilderness.

Moses heard their murmuring and scolded them, and

he went to seek the counsel of the Lord, and the Lord said, Tell the people not to fear, and Moses went before the people and told them not to fear and that the Lord would save them.

On the morrow they journeyed on and when they arrived at the Red Sea, God parted the waters for them, and they crossed on dry land and arrived on the other side and were safe, and during the night, when the Egyptians arrived, God returned the waters to their place and the sea rose up and covered the Egyptians and they and all their horses were drowned.

The people saw it, and they wept; they saw God's handiwork in their salvation, and faint with love and joy, they began to sing, and Moses also sang of his love for the Lord, saying,

>Who is like unto thee, O Lord, among the mighty?
>Who is like unto thee, in glory and holiness?
>The Lord shall reign for ever and ever.

And Miriam, his sister, took up her tambourine, and the women, seeing her, did likewise and took up theirs, and they danced around her as she sang,

>Sing to the Lord, almighty, exalted,
>The horse and his rider have the Lord thrown into the sea.

The Israelites journeyed on, following the cloud that was the Lord, and they wandered from Succoth to Migdol and from there to Sinai and from there to Jot-

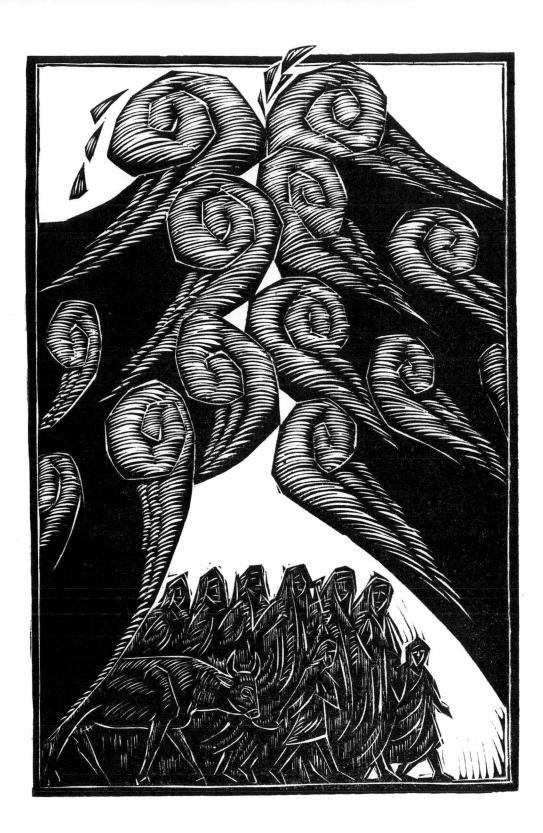

bah, and wherever they journeyed and wherever they encamped they saw the handiwork of the Lord.

In Marah, where the waters were bitter, God made the waters sweet for them.

In Massah, where there was no water, Moses drew water from a stone for them.

When they hungered, God sent them quail to eat in the evening and the thin bread they called manna to eat in the morning, and they had food.

And when enemies rose up against them and came from one direction, God scattered and confounded them and they fled in seven directions.

Again and again the Israelites did witness the handiwork of the Lord, yet they were not content and they began to complain about their long wandering and about the thin bread that they had to eat, and they began to long for the fish and cucumbers and melons and leeks and onions, and the other good food that they ate in Egypt.

Moses heard them and scolded them and the anger of God was kindled against them and God appeared to Moses and said, How long will they not believe in me? How long will I bear this evil congregation that keeps murmuring against me?

God punished the murmurers and they were destroyed, and God told Moses to assemble all the elders and nobles and priests in the tent of meeting, and when they assembled God filled the tent with the spirit of the Lord and when the people saw it they bowed down.

God renewed with the generation in the wilderness the covenant that had been made with Abraham and Sarah and Isaac and Rebecca and Jacob and Rachel and Leah, saying, Whosoever keeps the covenant shall be my treasure, for all the world is mine.

In awe and rapture the people listened to the voice of God speak the words of the law, saying,

> I am the Lord your God, who brought you out of Egypt, out of the house of bondage.
>
> You shall have no other gods before me.
>
> You shall not use the name of the Lord in vain.
>
> Keep the Sabbath holy, as the Lord your God has commanded you to do. Six days you shall labor, and do all your work, but the seventh day is the Sabbath of the Lord. In it you

28

shall not do any work, nor any member of your household, nor your servants, nor your beasts, nor the stranger who is within your gates.

    Honor your father and your mother.

    You shall not murder.

    You shall not commit adultery.

    You shall not steal.

    You shall not bear false witness.

    You shall not covet your neighbor's possessions.

Trembling before the presence of the Lord, the people bowed down their heads and answered, All that the Lord has spoken, we will do.

And the Lord commanded Moses to go up on Mount Sinai to receive the written law, saying, Come up, and I will give you the law, written on tablets of stone, that you may teach it to the children of Israel.

And Moses went up, and was away for forty days and forty nights, and at the end of that time God gave him the law, written on two tablets of stone, in God's hand, and saying, Speak to the children of Israel and let those whose hearts are willing build a sanctuary to the Lord that I may dwell among them, and God told Moses what should be built, how it should be built, who should build it, and stipulated the weight and measure of each thing and named also the materials that should be used, and said, Tell the children of Israel to keep my sabbaths, for it is a sign between them and me, a perpetual covenant between us, for in six days the Lord made heaven and earth, and on the seventh day the Lord rested.

Moses departed, and went down, and when he arrived at the camp and saw that the people had already forgotten the Lord, that they had melted down their rings and bracelets and made a golden calf to worship, and that they were worshipping it before the fire, Moses cast the tablets of stone out of his hand, breaking them, and he threw the golden calf into the fire.

The wrath of God was hot against the people and, in discourse with Moses, God spoke of annihilating them and starting a new race, but Moses pleaded for the people, saying, These were the children of Israel whom you saved from bondage, and to whom you have promised a land.

God caused those who worshipped the golden calf to be destroyed, and spared the rest. Then God commanded Moses to hew out two tablets of stone, like the first two, and to return to the mount, and Moses went up and was gone for forty days and forty nights, writing on the stones the words which God gave him to write, and when the writing was done, Moses went down with the law.

When the people saw that his face was radiant, they knew the spirit of God was upon him, and they were afraid to draw near.

Moses spoke to them, saying, These are the words which the Lord has commanded. Six days shall work be done but the seventh day shall be to you a holy day, a

Moses, now old, came before the people and said, Hear, O Israel, the Lord is God, the Lord is one.

And the people answered, saying, Blessed is the Lord.

And Moses recounted to them their long passage in the wilderness and reminded them that they had been disbelievers and that they had rebelled against the Lord and the Lord had tested them to see whether they would keep the commandments, and he warned them not to forget the Lord, saying, Love God with all your heart, with all your soul and with all your might. Teach these words to your children, and to your children's children.

The people wept, and they answered, Yea. And Moses reminded them of the perpetual covenant that was between them and the Lord, saying, Observe the Sabbath, to keep it holy. And they answered, Yea.

After forty years of wandering Moses died in the wilderness, and the people mourned for him and held him dear, for their ancestors Abraham and Sarah and Isaac and Rebecca and Jacob and Rachel and Leah had seen the presence of God but only Moses had seen the face of the Lord. They mourned for thirty days, but every seventh day they rested, and they kept the Sabbath holy.

And they journeyed on to the Promised Land, where they did arrive, and it was a good land, a land of milk and honey, a garden which brought forth a multitude of plants and trees, whose fruits were good to eat and a delight to behold.

35

They rejoiced in the land, and in the Lord who gave them the land, and they kept the Sabbath holy, resting on it, as the Lord had done. And the generations that kept it found a foretaste of paradise in it, as when longing for its arrival, the pious ones of Safed put on white robes on the eve of each sixth day and went up and down the hills chanting a welcome to the Sabbath and calling, Beloved.

As instructed by Moses, the Israelites have kept the Sabbath in all generations and have taught their children to keep it and their children have taught their children to keep it, unto this day.

It is kept for the Lord's sake and for their own sake, for they find the Sabbath a delight, and hasten, as evening approaches on each sixth day, to leave behind the

ordinary days of the week in order to prepare for the holiest day of the week, the queen of days, the Sabbath queen.

While it is still daylight, the house is scrubbed clean, the table is attractively set with the best china and silver that a family possesses, and unlit candles are placed on the table along with a *halla* bread, the traditional twisted Sabbath loaf. Two Sabbath meals, which must be superior to the other meals of the week, have been cooked and will be kept warm on a stove that will remain lit until the Sabbath is over.

At the moment of nightfall, the members of the family who are at home gather around the person, often a woman, who prepares to welcome the Sabbath in. Standing before unlit candles, she says: *Lord of the universe, I am about to perform the sacred duty of kindling the lights in honor of the Sabbath, even as it is written, and you shall call the Sabbath a delight.*

And may the effect of my fulfilling this commandment be that the stream of abundant life and heavenly blessing flow in upon me and mine, that thou be gracious unto us, and cause thy presence to dwell among us.

Continue thy loving-kindness unto me and my dear ones, make us worthy to walk in thy way, loyal to thy Torah and clinging to good deeds. Keep far from us all manner of shame, grief, and care, and grant that peace, light, and joy ever abide in our home, for with thee is the fountain of life, in thy light do we see light.

Listeners answer, Amen.

She then strikes a match and kindles the candles, adding, *Blessed is the Lord our God who has honored us with the commandment to kindle the lights of the Sabbath.*

The candles are now lit, and as the flames flicker into steadiness the presence of the Sabbath can be felt entering the home, bathing it in a warm glow and giving those present the feeling that they have been endowed with an extra, or Sabbath, soul.

In the synagogue, at the moment of nightfall, the family members who have gone there to pray chant in an introduction to worship: *Come, let us sing before the Lord, let us shout for joy to the holy presence, for the Lord is a great God, and a great king above all gods. The deep places of the earth belong to the Lord, and the high mountains are the Lord's, and the sea and the dry land were also formed by the Lord. Come, let us worship and bow down, let us kneel before the Lord, our Maker, for the Lord is our God.*

And they welcome the Sabbath with a song of love whose opening words are: *Come, our beloved, we greet thee with praise, welcome, Bride Sabbath, queen of all days.*

In song and prayer, the Lord is blessed and creation is praised, and the Oneness of God as the one and only power at work in the universe—a power that has no beginning and no end—is affirmed with the words: *Hear, O Israel: The Lord is God, the Lord alone.*

They proclaim the sovereignty of God in all matters and over all of life. Spiritually awakened and having acquired an extra soul, the Sabbath soul, in the course of prayer, they return home, calling out as they enter, *Shabat Shalom,* or *Gut Shabbos,* or Good Sabbath. *Shabat Shalom,* the family answers back.

Before sitting down at the table, they greet with song the Sabbath angels, the messengers of the most high, and bless the Lord, the supreme king of kings.

40

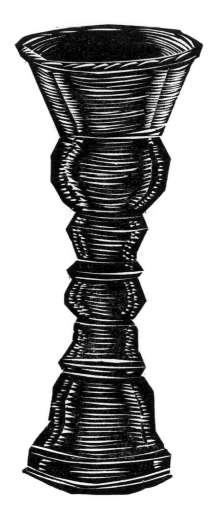

They bless the children, saying: *The Lord bless thee and keep thee, may the face of the Lord shine upon thee, and be gracious unto thee, may the face of the Lord turn unto thee, and give thee peace.*

Over a cup of wine, and formally ushering the Sabbath into the home, they say the *kiddush: And it was evening and it was morning—the sixth day, and the*

heaven and earth were finished. God rested on the seventh day, and called it holy because the work of creation was completed on that day.

Blessed art thou, O Lord our God, ruler of the universe, who created the fruit of the vine. Blessed art thou, O Lord our God, ruler of the universe, who has taken pleasure in us and given us thy commandments, and given us thy holy Sabbath as an inheritance, a memorial to creation, it being also the first of the holy convocations made with our ancestors when we were led out of Egypt. Blessed art thou, O Lord, who calls the Sabbath holy.

All then sit down to partake of the first of the Sabbath meals and if a stranger has appeared in their midst, the meal must be shared with the stranger, for no one may be permitted to spend the Sabbath alone.

Thanks are given for the food as it is eaten, each thing in turn being blessed, and the Lord who made the world and all that is in it, who made the miracle of creation is blessed, and after the meal table hymns are sung.

43

The following morning, when worshippers return to the synagogue, the ark is opened, the Torah is taken out and read, and adorations to the Lord are chanted and sung, to God of history, God of nature, God the creator of all life, God the healer of all flesh, God who is without beginning and without end, and they sing, *Holy, holy, holy is the Lord, the whole earth is full of the glory of the Lord.*

When prayers are ended, the second Sabbath meal is enjoyed at home. A feeling of peace and gladness prevails—until later in the day when the first three stars appear in the sky, signaling that night has arrived and that it is time to usher the Sabbath out.

Returning to the synagogue in the evening, they sing, *The Lord is a great God, a great king above all gods, and beside the Lord we have no king,* and, honoring the Lord, who gives them life, they chant: *We shall extol thee forever, Creator of all things, O God who every day opens the gates of the east, leading forth a sun from his place, and the moon from hers, giving light to the world and all its inhabitants.*

Exultantly, they proclaim the Oneness of God, who was, who is, and who will ever be, and they sing to the Lord, who is their ruler and king, the keeper of their lives, the master of their souls, whose many miracles they witness daily.

The ceremony of parting with the Sabbath in the synagogue is over, but the final parting is reserved for the home, so that all members of the family may escort the Sabbath out together.

After the third Sabbath meal has been eaten, all gather together for the *havdalah*—separation ceremony. A twisted havdalah candle is lit, the spice box is taken up, and over a cup of wine held in the hand one says: *Behold, God is my salvation, I will trust, and will not be afraid, for God the Lord is my strength, my song, and my salvation. The Lord is with us. The God of*

45

Jacob is our refuge. I lift up the cup of salvation and call upon the name of the Lord. Blessed art thou, O Lord our God, king of the universe, who has created the fruit of the vine.

The spice box is passed around for everyone to smell, and the words said are: *Blessed art thou, O Lord our God, ruler of the universe, who created all manner of spice.* Then, turning to the flame of the candle, they add: *Blessed art thou, O Lord our God, ruler of the universe, who created the light of the fire.*

The cup of wine is raised: *Blessed art thou, O Lord our God, ruler of the universe, who makes a distinction between holy and profane, between light and darkness, between Israel and heathen nations, between the seventh day and the six working days.*

The cup is passed around and each one sips from it. The candle is snuffed out, the spice box is returned to the shelf, and coins are put into a charity box by the children.

Another day of rest is ended, and a new round of ordinary days is about to begin. On the eve of the next sixth day, the Sabbath will once more be welcomed by those who keep it, and the queen of days will yet again be ushered in.

In this manner is the Sabbath kept. It has been kept as a sign between the Israelites and the Lord for thousands of years. And the words of the Lord, saying, Whosoever keeps the covenant shall be my treasure, for all the world is mine, those words are lived by the men and

46

women who keep the covenant, for as they rest on the Sabbath, their senses quicken to the marvels that the earth puts forth, which are good to eat, and fragrant, and pleasing to behold, and to the sun that warms from above, and to the bird that offers up its song, and they experience a portion of the delights of the garden of long ago.

As Moses had instructed, the Sabbath has been taught, and the covenant is kept as a sign between the Israelites and the Lord.